I0693645

Readiness 101

Being Disaster Ready without Becoming a Prepper

By: G. Peltz

This book is dedicated to the victims of Hurricanes Harvey, Irma, and Maria with my sincerest apologies for not having written it sooner.

Contents

Foreword

By this point in time, I'm sure everyone has heard of "Preppers". Preppers are those people who have stockpiled guns, ammunition, food and water in the expectation that the end of the world or at least the collapse of society is imminent. They have hidden fallout shelters, or cabins in the woods. They have four-wheel drives with lift kits and extra fuel tanks, and they're frequently telling everyone else that you need to get ready because one day Godzilla is going to come and destroy everything and then what are you going to do?

Now, I'm not saying preppers are crazy. Heck, I'm not even saying they're wrong. All that I am saying is that there are preppers out there.

This book is not for them.

This book is for absolutely everyone else. Because preppers have probably done everything in this book ten times over...at least. No, they probably don't need this book. In fact, I am quite sure that they would tell you this book doesn't go far enough.

But if you have a family, or live in a home, or breathe, well then one day, you just might need this book. Because whether it's the end of the world, or just the storm of the decade, sooner or later you are going to have a day that is just not going to be normal. And on that day, the superstores will be closed, the grocery stores will be closed, the greasy clowns will be closed...and if they're not, even if all of those places are somehow still open, you just might not be able to get to them.

I live on an island. It is not an island in the traditional sense, since no one would think of it as an island, and no one calls it an island. It's not in a lake, or the ocean, and it's not in the middle of a major river. But the fact is that I cannot get more than two miles in any direction from my house without crossing over water. By the technical definition this means that I do, in fact, live on an island. And in 2011 this fact was made very clear to me when I realized that thanks to the biggest flood our area had seen in 39 years, I couldn't get more than two miles from my house. And then the power went out.

That's when this book was conceived. Unfortunately, it was a very long gestation period, and the labor pains didn't start until some of my friends and family were forced to evacuate from the path of Hurricane Harvey in Texas in 2017. It was only then that I finally sat down and started writing.

Safety Information and Disclaimer

The purpose of this book is to present you with some basic "common sense" survival techniques to help you be more prepared in the event of a disaster than you might currently be. Nothing about this book or the information contained within is designed to encourage you to stay put when an evacuation has been ordered, or even suggested. Evacuation is almost always the safest bet when you have forewarning of a disaster approaching. Please follow all safety recommendations of your local governmental agencies, police, fire and rescue or local news. If they say to get out, please get out. Everything you leave behind is replaceable, but your life is not.

The purpose of this book is not to give you instructions on surviving a specific type of disaster. It is strictly a book about being prepared to survive the effects common to many disaster scenarios, such as not having access to food and water, living without public utilities for a period of time, and holding out on your own until either civilization is restored or you can be rescued and moved to a safer place.

While I do possess several FEMA certifications and I do have training in disaster preparedness and reaction there is no way I can know the exact nature or extent of your situation. The local authorities will be better informed, and will know which roads are open, which hospitals are operating during the crisis, where shelters may have been established and what resources are available. Please defer to these sources before you rely on any books you may have read, including this one. By the way, a quick web search will find you a ton of additional information from FEMA including their disaster preparedness guide. Some of the things I say will be in that guide. Other things I say may actually seem to conflict with that guide. Even so, I strongly encourage you to download and read that guide as well. Then you can make your own informed decisions before a disaster happens to you. This book is strictly my opinion, and is intended for informational purposes only. I strongly encourage you to seek additional education on the topics discussed here.

The safest place to be during any disaster is somewhere else. That may sound like a joke, but it is true. If you know a disaster or potential disaster is approaching, please seriously consider evacuating. If you can be somewhere else when a disaster strikes, that is almost always the safest option. Riding out a disaster should always be your last choice.

About this Book

The purpose of this book is to teach you a common sense approach to being prepared for a disaster scenario. It is not designed to teach you how to survive the actual disaster itself. That is an entirely separate issue, and each type of disaster could have an entire book dedicated just to survival in that scenario alone. Most books I have seen on disaster preparedness seem to be aimed at the hardcore survivalist. They're full of fire starting tips, and freeze dried food recommendations. This is all great information if you are preparing for the complete collapse of society. For the average person this simply is not realistic. Why spend all that money and effort on enough food and supplies to start a new civilization when realistically most disaster victims only have to fend for themselves for 24-72 hours?

Now, if you live in an extremely remote area, the extreme survival scenario might actually be appropriate for you. Are you in the Alaskan wilderness? Are you living on a remote island? Are you out in Appalachia somewhere in the backwoods where it always takes days or even weeks before someone comes out to fix your power outages? If you answered yes to any of these questions, or you think you live in a similarly remote or wild area, it might be a good idea to prepare to hold out for months at a time. But for the average person, this is just not usually the case. Besides, if you are living one of those lifestyles, you probably already know quite a bit about being self-sustaining.

The typical disaster generally resolves the main cause fairly quickly. Winds from a tornado generally last only minutes, people in the path of hurricanes experience wind and rain for usually no more than a day or two at most, and snowstorms usually end after a few hours. What most people truly need to be prepared to survive is the aftermath and cleanup. It can take days to get power restored, streets plowed and passable, or for flood waters to recede. This book is about surviving that time it takes society to get back at least to functional, even if normal may still be a long way off.

No, the average person doesn't need twenty cases of military grade MREs (Meals Ready to Eat) to get through three or four days stuck in the house without power. In fact, many people already have everything they need to survive through that time right in their kitchen and their linen closet. Got a can of peas, a bottle of water and a blanket? Look at you, you're already halfway to being survivalist!

This book is all about an everyday approach to survival. We will do almost all of our shopping in the normal grocery store, and we will be eating (mostly, anyway) the same foods we eat every day. The book will be divided into three sections. Section 1 is about surviving at home. Section 2 is about being prepared at work or school (without even making your coworkers or classmates think you're a freak!), and Section 3 will be about surviving on your commute. I strongly encourage you to read all three sections, even if you don't work or work from home. Some of the tips in Sections 2 and 3 can come in handy even when shopping, visiting friends, or travelling.

Let me start off with the most important tip of them all:

1. Ask yourself, "Is this actually a disaster?" That may sound like a weird or even inconsiderate thing to say, but seriously think about it. Is this actually a disaster? Read on.

In 2011 two hurricanes moved through my area. These two hurricanes were named Irene and Lee. Now, I live in Pennsylvania (in the United States). Pennsylvania is not particularly known for being hurricane prone, but every few years one reaches us. In my area one of these hurricanes brought record flooding. I believe that was Lee, and is the story mentioned earlier that made me realize I live on an island. The other hit my area with hurricane winds, but we were on the fringes and got almost no rain. We did lose power, though. A call to our power company informed us that we would be without power for three days.

In my neighborhood a lot of people were standing out in the streets talking, so I naturally joined in. Many of them were concerned about how they were going to get through three days with no electricity. It was late August, it was warm and it was sunny. No one was worried too much about heat or anything like that. There wasn't a lot of natural gas in our area at the time, and pretty much everyone had an electric stove. They were concerned with how they were going to cook their food.

I laughed, and they all looked at me like I was crazy. I looked at them and pointed out something they were all over looking. This was suburbia. Every single one of us had a barbeque grill. Our disaster shortly turned into a sort of impromptu block party, with everyone grilling and sharing food with their neighbors. The power actually ended up being restored the next day.

Even during the flooding my neighborhood was high and dry. We had power, we had water, and the rain stopped after the first day. Other than not being able to go anywhere, it wasn't really much of a disaster for us. Now, the power did go out later due to a switching station being damaged by flood waters, but it was only out for a few hours. The biggest issue that time was that even though we were fine, the water purification plant was flooded and they shut down all water to our area.

This is what I mean by an everyday, common sense approach to disaster survival. No electricity, use your grill (outside only! No grilling indoors!). No refrigeration? Eat canned food. And this is why the first question to ask yourself is, "Is this really a disaster?" By the time you finish this book you will probably be able to answer "No" to that question more often than you might think.

Just a couple of generations ago no one considered it a disaster if they were flooded in, or snowed in or had no power for a few days. As long as the house was still standing, they knew they would be fine. They knew this because of the way they lived. When there wasn't a superstore within fifteen minutes of everyone's home, and no one used drones to deliver groceries you ordered on the internet, people were actually better prepared than we are now. They had a way to heat their houses and they had their pantries fully stocked at all times. And that was all it took to get by for them.

Well, that's all it will take to get by for you, too. An alternate source of warmth, a ready supply of food and water, and the confidence of knowing you are prepared. Those are the main tools you will need to get through almost anything that may happen.

The second most important tip of all would be this:

2. Have a home evacuation plan. Too many people don't bother with this, and yet thousands of

homes catch fire every year. Flash floods can cause people to be forced to leave quickly. Trees can fall on houses and turn them into an unstable pile of sticks that needs to be evacuated. Do you know how you would get out if your front door was on fire? What if your whole family is asleep on the second floor when the stairs collapse in an earthquake? An evacuation plan for the place you spend over half of your life is essential. And practice the plan. I know having a fire drill at home seems silly, but isn't it even sillier that you're better prepared to escape from work or school than you are from your own house? Oh, and make sure you have blankets or coats or something for once you are outside. These items, and maybe even clothes for everyone could be packed in a bag near the fire escape, or out in the trunk of your car (we'll discuss that more in Section 3), or stored in a deck box or the shed somewhere. If using outside storage, consider vacuum bags, or at least zipper bags to keep everything dry and pest free. Then you won't be standing out in the rain in your pajamas and bare feet while you wait for the firefighters to do their jobs.

I'm not trying to make you feel guilty here, but maybe you should. Seriously, how would you feel knowing you lost your family just because you thought having a fire drill at home was silly? And don't stop at knowing how to get out of the house. Have a plan on where to stay if the house is unlivable for a short time. Have a plan if it is unlivable for a long time. Have a plan if you need to leave the area for a few days, or weeks, or more. Evacuation without a destination is just running away blindly. That may save you in the moment, but then what? You need to plan.

Why do I Need to Prepare?

So you may be asking yourself, "Why do I need to prepare? I'm not one of these people who think that the government is going to collapse, or that the world is going to end. What is there for me to prepare for?"

Well, that is a fair enough question. But as I sit here writing this in the fall of 2017, there are hundreds of thousands of people in the United States of America who have been displaced or otherwise impacted by three major hurricanes in just two weeks and by wildfires in the Northwest and in the Napa Valley region. Those who evacuated now have to wait for days, weeks or in some cases even months before they will be able to return to their homes, if they even have a home to return to. Those who did not evacuate may now find themselves without power, without clean drinking water and without local facilities such as grocery stores and restaurants being opened again for a similar amount of time.

Do you know what would happen to you in this situation? How are you going to eat, drink and survive until the world around you gets back to normal? Even if that only takes a few days, are you really ready for that? Do you have a family? How would you feed your family? How would you keep them warm? How would keep them alive?

Maybe you don't live in the regular path of hurricanes. So maybe you think you don't have to worry about such devastation. While it may be true that the largest number of people affected by a natural disaster is usually the result of a hurricane (or typhoon, or monsoon) this is due to the sheer size of these storms. But they are far from the only forces of nature that can devastate an area and shut down your way of life for a time. Tornados, earthquakes, tsunamis, landslides, snowstorms, floods, wildfires and a host of other natural disasters force people from their homes every year. Dam breaks, plant explosions, chemical spills and fires, terrorist attacks, wars, riots and power grid failures are just some of the manmade calamities that can upset your normal routine. Even things as simple as a strike by grocery store workers, delivery truck drivers, utility workers or farmers could potentially put you into a situation where your normal way of doing things just won't work.

There are individual disasters as well. What if your roof caves in, or your furnace goes out in the middle of a snowstorm? What if you discover toxic mold in your walls? What if someone crashes into the transformer down the street and you're going to be without power for a few days?

Even a small disaster can potentially lead to several days where you're normal life can get turned upside down. If you aren't prepared for it, it can be that much more devastating. That being said, we'll start the tips off with reasons why you should be prepared.

The Tips

3. You want to live. This may sound like I am being facetious or overly dramatic, but really this is the most important reason to be prepared. During almost any disaster a percentage of the people killed are people who simply either weren't prepared, or didn't heed the warnings.

4. You have people who count on you. Your family may be counting on you to protect them from whatever the world may throw at them, especially if you have young children. So, even if

for some reason number 3 isn't true, consider those around you.

5. If you're not prepared, you place an added burden on everyone else. If you fail to complete even the most basic preparation for what may happen, then when something does happen you will become a part of the problem. Rescuers have to find and save you, neighbors have to share their supplies (well, they don't *have* to, but they may feel obligated) and local resources like fire or police departments that could be fixing infrastructure or dealing with those who can't help themselves now have to be dedicated to saving you. Don't become a burden. Be prepared.

6. Because disasters happen. This is a simple fact of life in our world. Just look at the news. Wildfires and landslides, earthquakes and hurricanes, terror attacks and hackers...these things are in the news almost daily it seems. And anyone of them or a dozen other events could shut down life as we know it, at least temporarily.

7. Because being prepared saves money. Seriously. If you are prepared for the situation then you

may be protected from price gouging, or being forced to stay in a hotel or who knows what other expenses caused by being hard hit. And (especially if you follow this book) some basic preparations are way cheaper than you might think.

8. It doesn't make you some "crazy doomsday prepper" just because you're ready to take care of yourself and your loved ones in the case of a disaster. This book isn't about preparing for the end of the world. It's about preparing for realistic tragedies that happen from time to time.

Section 1

Being prepared at Home

I said earlier that I was going to tell you how to be prepared at home, at work or school, and on the road. This first section will discuss being prepared at home. Many of these tips will actually translate to work or school and even to on the road in smaller scale. Never the less, I will go over each section separately for the sake of convenience and ease of separating the lists.

The Absolute Basics

Hopefully you will never have to face a disaster. If you are lucky enough for that to be the case, then the steps in this book will have resulted in nothing more than you becoming somewhat more organized, and with a minimal amount of time, effort and money invested in the process. On the other hand, if a tragedy should strike, some simple preparations will make it that much easier for you to get through it.

The most common disasters are usually fairly short term. You might get snowed in for a couple of days, or flooding might cut you off from the rest of the world for a day or two. Maybe you had a warning that it was coming, and ran to the grocery store. Maybe you didn't have any such warning, and now you're stuck in the house without having done the obligatory "eggs-bread-and-milk" run. I am not sure if this is a global phenomenon or just a localized thing, but here where I live every time a major storm of any sort is called for, or in the case of snow, anything over a half an inch, people rush to the grocery stores and buy up all of the bread, milk and eggs. I guess most people around here must eat a lot of French toast during a disaster.

There are some basic things that you should have ready in case of a disaster. Many of these things seem to be forgotten in this day and age, but most of them are things everyone used to have handy.

The Tips

9. Remember back in Tip 2 I said "Have a Plan"? Well, make sure everyone knows the plan. How in depth to go with each family member, coworker, friend, etc. will require using your own judgement. For example, your spouse or roommate should probably know every detail. Your six year old on the other hand really only needs the basics and it should be explained in a way that reassures them that your family is prepared, rather than a way that makes them scared that a disaster could happen at any moment. Wait until they're older before you tell them how scary the world is. And seriously consider having a drill once in a while. Maybe every six to twelve months. And actually evaluate those drills to see what you should

change, or what everyone might need clearer instructions on.

10. Get at least one escape ladder for occupied second floors. In most places if a third floor (or higher) is occupied, a permanent fire escape is required by code. If not, ensure those floors have escape ladders as well. These can be rope or chain, and the higher quality ones permanently attach to a wall below the window. If you need to get out, you open the window, drop the ladder out, and climb down. Make sure everyone knows how to use it.

11. Get a fire extinguisher. Get two. Or even three. Make sure they are ABC extinguishers so they can be used on all types of fires. Make sure that you have one in your kitchen, and that this one is dry chemical. Spraying any kind of liquid onto a grease fire is never a good idea. Again, learn how to use it. No tool is ever going to do you any good if you can't use it. I'm not saying go spray down your stove with a fire extinguisher here, but read the directions, know how the pin is attached, know how the trigger works, know where to aim and how far away to stand.

12. Are you, or is anyone in your family under
    medical care? Do you have allergies, asthma,
    high blood pressure or a heart condition? If you
    or anyone you care for is taking medications
    daily, never wait until the last minute to refill
    those prescriptions. If you only have one pill left
    when a flood traps you at home for a week, it's
    going to be a rough week. If your kid's inhaler is
    empty when the power goes out for three days,
    the results could be far more devastating than
    the original power failure. Please, be prepared in
    advance. And make sure you rotate this supply
    as well. Many medications lose their
    effectiveness when they expire, and some can
    even become toxic.

13. Know what disasters your area is prone to. Do
    you live near a railroad that transports
    chemicals? Are you smack dab in the middle of
    the American mid-west's infamous "tornado
    alley"? Are you on the Southeastern US' or Gulf
    of Mexico's coast? Are landslides or wildfires
    common in your region? Does that river right
    down the road flood often? Has the nearby
    chemical depot had any leaks? You should know
    what can hit your area.

14. Know the history. One of the best ways to know what *can* happen is to know what already *did* happen. If tornadoes have hit your area in the past, there is a fairly good chance that they will hit again. A friend of mine once had to leave Colorado to go help his parents after 90 inches of snow fell in Buffalo, New York where they lived. 90 inches of snow! That's 7 and a half feet of snow! And guess what? It wasn't even a record. They've had more snow than that on the ground there in the past. Has that happened where you live? Check your local history. Know what has happened before, and you're likely to be better prepared for what could happen again.

15. Know the warning signs. Pay attention to weather forecasts, and know a "watch" from a "warning", or a "chance of" from a "we're keeping an eye on it" situation. Know what different alarms and sirens in your area mean. Is that loud siren you just heard the volunteer fire department, or a tornado warning, or is the local nuclear power plant in meltdown? Check you city's/town's/borough's web page. Ask the neighbors. Find the local library. Search the internet. As Chris Carter used to make David

Duchovny remind us every week, "The truth is out there."

16. Have a designated safe place in your home. This should be away from windows and near structural support such as a load bearing wall. Ideally this place should have access to a closet and a bathroom. This is especially important in tornado or earthquake prone areas where structural damage is most likely to occur. In a basement near an external wall with a door to the outside might just be perfect for this, so long as there is no danger of flooding. If it is not in a basement, you should stay away from external walls. You can also purpose build, or have purpose built such a space if you're in a very high risk area.

17. Make sure there are a smoke detector (with battery power) and a Carbon Monoxide detector (with battery power) in the safe place. If you have anything in your house that runs on natural gas, have a gas detector installed there as well. If installing them yourself remember that smoke detectors go up high and gas detectors go down low (follow all manufacturer's directions on installation and use). CO detectors can go either

high or low because CO is roughly the same density as normal atmosphere. If your safe place is in the basement consider a radon alarm as well. Even if you get the house tested (and you really should get the house tested) and they say it's clean an earthquake could stir things up, or flood saturated soil could start releasing the gasses trapped within.

18. Make sure your safe place is clean. Clean it on a regular basis, and ensure it is rodent and insect free. Even the most generous among us is likely to find rats and spiders sharing our disaster shelter to be a little over the top.

19. Have a way to heat this space. Even warm climates can get cold sometimes. Being prepared to last for days without outside assistance won't matter at all if you succumb to hypothermia while you're waiting for the world to become habitable again. Make sure your heating method will work even with no power, and that it is approved for indoor use. There are propane and kerosene heaters designed for indoor use. Be sure to read and follow all directions and safety information. Be sure to keep these heaters well away from kids, pets and flammable materials.

Keep them well maintained and in operating order, and keep a supply of the appropriate fuel on hand and stored properly. And again, especially if you're using heaters, have smoke, CO and gas detectors in the area.

20. Have blankets handy in your safe place, or even better, have sleeping bags. Maybe consider pillows and jackets as well. And have extras, especially of blankets. You may want to use them to cover doorways or windows to make it easier to keep your safe place warm and dry. The smaller the space, the easier it will be to keep that space warm. In case of a failure of your heat source, or if you don't have a heat source, using blankets to build a tent fort will help trap body heat in. The smaller the space, the easier it will be to keep warm.

21. Find a dry, out-of-the-way place to store your supplies. Also, make sure that place is at least well enough temperature controlled to prevent freezing. This could be a pantry, a closet in the living room, a shelf in the basement...any place that your kit isn't going to be in the way, but you will still be able to access it quickly. Ideally this storage place and your safe place should be

together. If that is not practical have your emergency supplies in a bag or box or footlocker…something you can easily grab and take along to your safe place.

22. Know your neighbors! Many people these days don't even know their own neighbors. Now I'm not saying you have to play pinochle, or even have them over for a bar-b-que, but if you at least know each other's names and phone numbers you can look after each other a little better. Of course, going the extra step and actually becoming friends with them might just be in everyone's best interest. After all, friends are even more likely to look out for each other in tough times. Plus, honestly what's the point of living in a neighborhood if you're not going to be neighborly?

23. Write down a list of phone numbers. Thanks to cell phones and storing numbers and people doing everything online instead of over the phone, many people no longer write down or memorize phone numbers. Of course everyone knows to call 911 (or 999 in most of Europe) for an emergency. But what if it's not an emergency? What if you need to reach the

police, or fire department but it's not a matter of life or death? You just look up the number on your cell phone, right? What if the towers are down, or the network is busy? What if your cell phone gets broken or wet? Do you know your mother's phone number? If you have a loved one in long term care, do you know the facility's number? How about your spouse's work or your kids' schools? What if you have to call the power company and get on the list for an outage repair? How about your homeowner's or renter's insurance company? Get these numbers and write them down. Keep them in your wallet, on your fridge, and with your survival supplies. Store them in your cell phone as well, but if your phone gets lost or damaged, you're going to need that written copy. Laminate it or keep it in a watertight bag (like a zipper sandwich bag).

24. Use those numbers. Call mom and tell her you're alive. Even if you're a terrible son or daughter and don't care that she's worried, at least it'll keep her from calling your fire and police departments five hundred times to track you down and tying up their phone lines. Call your neighbors, both to check on them, and to let

them know how you're doing. Or go next door and actually see how they're doing, if you can.

25. Trapped in the house? Call someone and tell them. Usually this means the fire department. Don't call 911 if it's not an emergency. They need that line open for real emergencies. This book is going to leave you prepared to deal with being trapped in the house for a day or two, but you still need to call them. Oh, and when you call, let them know that you are prepared to stay a few days (only if you are in fact are prepared, and no one is injured) so that they can prioritize and get to those who didn't read this book. If they do say they may be a day or two, ask them if they want you to check in, and how often. They may be surprised, in fact they will probably be very surprised, but they will really appreciate your level of readiness.

26. Call the power company and let them know if your service is out. They may be able to give you an idea when power will return, but more to the point they may not know you're area is out until you call. Let them know if you have any medical needs that require the power be back on. It may

change their priority or they may suggest you
evacuate.

27. If the power in your area goes out frequently, consider a household generator back up. A professionally installed whole house system could make it seem as though nothing happened. One that powers at least your furnace (even many gas and oil furnaces require the power be on to run), your hot water heater (if electric) and your refrigerator should really be enough though; you'll have to decide for yourself. Be sure to keep it properly fueled and maintained per the manufacturer's or installer's instructions.

28. If you don't lose power often enough to bother with the expense of a whole house system, consider a portable generator. Add up the requirements of the items you want to be able to keep running (refrigerator, furnace, well pump, etc.) and add some load for phone chargers, a couple of lamps, or some odds and ends, and get a generator that can handle that load plus a little more still. Make sure you have enough extension cords, and that they are approved for the load in question. You may have

to have an electrician come modify some equipment. For example, many furnaces are hard wired. By installing a cord and an outlet the electrician can set it up so you can hook up to the generator instead. The electrician can also probably help you determine just how much generator power you actually need. Just remember; never run a generator inside of any structure. Exhaust fumes are deadly, and can build up quickly.

29. If you have an alternate power source, such as solar with a battery backup, talk to your electrician about adding a generator that can recharge that battery bank. Storms can sometimes limit solar charging ability for days, or snow can cover panels. Depending on your system adding a generator to charge the cells may or may not be an option for you.

30. Call your homeowner's or renter's insurance company if you have damage. Also call the car insurance if you have damage to your car(s). They will probably be building a list of claims in your area and calling them early lets them get you on a list with other people in your area. If you wait too long to call the adjuster may have

already been through your area and now you will have to wait for them to come back around. Oh, and by the way…

31. Make sure you have insurance! I can't stress this enough. Even if you're a renter, you need insurance. The landlord isn't going to replace your belongings unless he or she caused the disaster somehow and you successfully sue them. Otherwise you need insurance. Your home is your biggest investment. And most of your smaller investments are inside of it. Make sure it is all covered for everything that may go wrong. Even if your area was high and dry when Noah built his ark, consider flood insurance. If it has never flooded, you may pay as little as a dollar a month. Without flood insurance nothing considered a flood by the insurance companies will be covered, and some insurance companies consider virtually all water damage to be a "flood". That can even include broken pipes or a leaking foundation.

32. Always have a flashlight close by. This is true in essentially every situation. Even if it is just a little key chain flashlight, keep one handy. Put one in your desk drawer at work, the glove box of your

car, your purse or brief case, your computer bag, or anywhere else you can think of. No, the flashlight app on your cell phone is not enough. You're going to want to keep that phone battery charged, and using the flashlight eats it up. And check the batteries regularly in all your flashlights. In my house I have several rechargeable automatic flashlights. They plug into an outlet and have a setting for nightlight and a setting for automatic. In automatic mode they actually sense a power failure and turn on like the emergency lights in commercial buildings. They can also be unplugged and carried around like a normal flashlight as well.

33. Have a spare battery or a charged up power pack for your cell phone. Then turn it off until you actually need it. You're going to regret all those hours playing Angry Birds when you can't call for help after three days with no sign of rescue.

34. Get a fire box. You'll have to choose one that suits your needs, but I recommend the brief case type. Ensure it is water proof as well as fire proof. Then put all of your important papers in it. Birth certificates, passports, social security cards, wills, advanced medical directives (living

wills), property titles/deeds and insurance
policies and cards should be the bare minimum.
Either originals or certified copies (where
allowed by law). All of these papers will be
extremely important if there is a major cleanup
or to prove identities and ownership after an
evacuation. Keep this case somewhere you can
grab it quickly if you need to evacuate, and
ideally near the rest of your survival supplies.

Water

The average human being will probably die in just three days without water. If it is extremely hot, or you are exerting yourself with manual labor it can be even shorter. The average human body needs as much as a gallon of water per day just to perform the normal tasks of breathing, digesting food and cleaning out the waste from your system. We tend not to realize how much water we use because it is so readily available, and because we get much of it in other forms. We get some water from other beverages such as coffee, soda or iced tea. We get some water from foods we eat, especially vegetables and soups.

When we don't get enough water in our bodies we start to experience dehydration. The early signs sometimes hit us even in day to day life without us realizing it. Muscle and stomach cramps, thirst and headache can all be signs of the early stages of dehydration. When dehydration starts to become more severe symptoms can start to include diarrhea, extreme muscle pain and fatigue, the loss of our body's ability to regulate temperature and even hallucinations. In extreme cases otherwise rational and sane people have been driven to the point of attempting to drink sewage, salt water, gasoline and other dangerous liquids just to attempt to quench the thirst.

In the United States, FEMA (the Federal Emergency Management Agency) recommends that you always have enough drinking water on hand to survive for three days. I would say that a better recommendation would be five days. Storing five days' worth of water may sound like a daunting task to some people; to others it may sound redundant. It all depends on how you normally get your water, and how aware you are of how much of it we use every day.

The Tips

35. The typical recommendation is for at least one gallon of water per person, per day. This makes storing water for a large family a rather tall order. Additionally it should be noted that this recommendation is strictly for consumption. It does not include water for cooking, cleaning, hygiene, etc.

36. If you are a bottled water drinker you can buy bottled water by the case, and stockpile it somewhere in your home or garage. Then when you go to the store you can buy new cases, and swap them out with the old. Use the older bottles for drinking, place the newer ones in storage. Roughly eight 500ml bottles (typical bottled water single serve size) equals 1 gallon. The bottles of this size may be labeled as 500ml, .5L or 16.9oz. This means a case of twenty four 500ml bottles is three gallons or a three day supply for one person. Every time you buy a new case, put the new case in the stockpile and take one of those cases out to be used for drinking. This will ensure the water doesn't get too old sitting around in storage.

37. Another option is to buy a water cooler for your house. You could get one of the office types with the five gallon bottles or I have seen one gallon and two gallon versions as well. This is frequently cheaper than buying individual bottles anyway. One of these coolers and a refillable bottle could not only help you be prepared, but it could save you money over buying single serve bottles as well. Often the big bottles for these tanks are sanitized and refilled

making it better for the environment as well. You could keep one (or more) five gallon bottles per person (or the equivalent amount of smaller bottles) in the house at all times, rotating these bottles the same way as we discussed for the smaller ones. Use a bottle from storage to load the cooler, put the new bottle in storage to replace it.

38. If you don't drink bottled water and don't want to use a water cooler, or if you have a very large household, consider buying a water barrel. These are large drums (usually blue plastic) with a spigot. They can be placed on a stand and then the spigot can be opened and closed to get water out as needed. Check the manufacturer's instructions as the drums will need to be emptied and sanitized from time to time. One of these barrels (or more) could also be used to keep extra water for cleaning and hygiene if you chose. Just remember these barrels are very heavy. A gallon of water weighs about 8 pounds and these typically hold 35-55 gallons.

39. Don't forget the animals when you are calculating how much water you will need to have stored. You will have to estimate how

much water Fido and Fluffy use. If you have no idea, stick with the gallon a day formula to be safe.

40. If you really insist on not buying water, then improvise. Fill containers on your own. Almost anything will work. You could buy empty five gallon jugs, and fill them from the tap. You could refill empty plastic soda or juice bottles with water as well. Just remember, especially since these containers aren't sealed and sterilized, make sure to dump them out, wash them well, and refill them at least once a month.

41. Whatever method of water storage you choose there are a couple of things to remember. You will want to store the water someplace that it won't freeze. You will want to be able to transport at least some of that water in case you are forced to evacuate. In many evacuation scenarios people end up stuck on the road for an extended time. We will go over being prepared for that situation in another section, but for now just consider that you will want to have your water (and food) with you if that should happen, so make sure at least some of it is mobile. You will also want to be able to get to your water

from the area where you are holding up. Water stored in a shed 100 meters from the house isn't of mush use if the snow is blocking all the exits.

42. A note about municipal water supplies: Municipal water supplies, or "city water" as we always called it when I was growing up, are usually (in the US at least) fed by water towers. The water is pumped up into a tower, and then gravity feeds it through all of the pipes and into your house. In bigger cities instead of a tower it is often a tank on the roof your building. This means that during power outages you will usually still have water until the tower or the tank runs dry. Without power the municipality cannot refill the tanks and towers, though, so eventually this water will run out as well. In most disaster scenarios this water, while it is still available, will most likely still be perfectly good, clean and potable water. It is possible, however, that the water supply could become tainted. This is especially true during floods, where dirty water can get mixed into the system through access points that have become submerged, and during earthquakes, where broken pipes can allow contaminants into the system. In cases where it has somehow become contaminated

the municipality will usually turn it off. Frequently they will also communicate this out through social media, traditional media and, if available in your area, reverse 911 calls. Check with your local services. Some areas still require that you register to receive reverse 911 calls. I have not seen any information on similar services outside of the US. I would suggest checking with local authorities or phone service providers no matter where you live. The point is, even though you may have access to municipal water during a disaster that supply might be limited, or it may get cut off. Depending on the nature of the disaster, it also may not be safe to consume even if it is readily available.

43. A note about well water: If you have well water then most likely you have an electric pump that delivers the water into your house. If you have power or if your well is attached to back-up power (a generator, batteries, etc.) then you should have water. Similarly to municipal water, though, it is possible for your water to become contaminated. Again this would be most likely to happen during a flood, especially if your pump and well cap end up underwater, or during earthquakes where sediment and debris can

litter the well. This can also happen if mining accidents or chemical spills affect the water tables. If any of these disasters should occur, or any other disaster I didn't think to include that could possibly threaten the water, you may want to not only use stored water instead, but also have your well water tested before returning to using it.

Food

While they say that the average person can survive without food for up to three weeks, I can tell you that trying to do so is not a pleasant experience. If you've ever missed even just one regular meal, you probably know that just being hungry is quite uncomfortable. As time goes on that discomfort will become greater and greater until you finally get to eat something. Eventually your insulin and glucose levels will get out of balance, and the body will store glucose in the blood stream instead of feeding it to the cells like it's supposed to. Then your body will start breaking down stored fat and protein reserves (usually that means muscle) in an attempt to feed itself. During this time you may become irritable, slow, and dizzy or feint, have muscle cramps and get easily confused. As the starvation continues the body loses large amounts of minerals and the electrical impulses that make our hearts beat and our brains work start to get interrupted.

Now, there is no clear timeline for these events to occur. It actually varies from person to person even with similar body masses and the same medical conditions. Of course, if you have food on hand you won't need to find out how long it takes for you.

Being prepared with food does not mean you have to stockpile beef jerky and military MREs or freeze dried survival foods. It does mean that you can't rely on your refrigerator and freezer (those will be discussed more in another section). Foods that don't require refrigeration will be our key source of nutrition if the power is out.

You don't have to head out to the outdoors super stores and buy camp food or survival food. Literally anything you already buy in the grocery store that doesn't need to be refrigerated is a perfectly acceptable choice for a disaster survival food. Anything with an extended shelf life, and especially if it doesn't require refrigeration even after opening is perfect. Anything from a can of corn to a jar of peanut butter, or even a box of crackers and a foil pack of tuna will be exactly what you need.

Just a note here, in the following section I talk a bit about "canned" foods. Three things I want to point out as you read this section. If you keep canned foods in your emergency kit, make sure to keep a can opener in your kit as well. While many modern cans have pull-ring tops, not all of them do. What's more, those rings can snap off leaving you in need of a can opener after all. The second point I want to make is that food in jars that don't require refrigeration is considered (by USDA definitions) to be "canned" food. The third point is that if you have canned food and the can is bulging outward, or if the lid on a jar is pushed upward from the inside then there is a very high probability that the food in that can has become infested with toxic bacteria, most likely *Clostridium Botulinum*. Discard any such cans or jars immediately upon their discovery. Starving may not sound like a great idea, but it's actually probably better than botulism. I can't say for sure, as I have personally never starved to death, but I have had botulism. I can tell you that personally, I will have to be one breathe from cannibalism before I choose to eat something that might give me that particular sickness again.

The Tips

44. When the power goes out the best thing to do with the refrigerator and freezer is to simply not touch them. Refrigerators and freezers are very well insulated. They will stay cold for quite a

while if they don't get opened. If the power is
out for more than a few hours, as soon as power
comes back check your food. If the frozen stuff is
still frozen solid, it should be perfectly safe. Use
a temperature probe or meat thermometer to
check your refrigerated foods. If they are above
40°F (5°C) then you should probably discard
them.

45. Get a good cooler. If the power has been out for
a few hours, or as soon as you find out that the
power is going to be out for a few days you can
save your cold foods by transferring them to a
cooler. Pack the frozen foods in the center as
tightly together as you can. This will help them
stay frozen longer. It's similar to how a large
block of ice melts more slowly than a smaller
one. Then put refrigerated foods around the
frozen food. If there is a lot of empty space, then
consider packing that space with newspaper or a
towel. Dead space will cause the food to warm
up faster.

46. If you are going to use your cold foods, use them
early. Have a temperature probe and check to be
certain they are still in the safe food range
(under 40°F or 5°C) before eating them. Don't

eat anything raw that wasn't meant to be eaten raw. If it needs cooked you will have to decide if your situation allows cooking at the time.

47. Fresh fruits and vegetables generally don't require refrigeration. I know everyone seems to think that they do, but they don't, although it does slow the ripening and rotting process. As long as the fruits or vegetables are whole, they won't spoil in just a few hours like some foods do. These will be perfectly acceptable foods to eat just as they would in any other circumstance. In fact, if you have advance warning of a possible disaster where you may need to shelter in place, buying fresh fruits and veggies beforehand should be a priority. Preferably ones that can be eaten raw in case cooking options are limited. Keep an eye on them for signs of mold or rot just as you should under normal circumstances. As a bonus, fresh fruit and vegetables may actually contribute to keeping your body hydrated as many of them contain large amounts of water.

48. Dried foods. I know I said earlier that you don't need to rely on beef jerky and freeze dried meals. Dried foods have the disadvantage of requiring extra water. Salted foods like jerky will

require drinking extra water to flush the salts from your system. Freeze dried meals, dry beans, dry rice and pasta all have the disadvantage of requiring water to be cooked in. If you have the water available, there is nothing wrong with these options, so I would be remiss if I did not include them here in the book. But if you have a limited water supply, leave this stuff on the shelf.

49. Dried fruit. Unlike most other dried foods, dried fruit is not completely devoid of water (unless you buy things like apple or banana chips that are actually crunchy). They won't replenish water like fresh fruit will, and due to the high fiber concentration they can lead to diarrhea if they are eaten in large quantities, especially by those who don't eat them regularly. But if they are eaten sparingly, or are already a staple in your diet, these are an excellent choice for a survival snack. Keep a few bags in your kit, and remember to cycle them out and eat them before they expire.

50. Trail mix. A good trail mix is packed with high calorie, high vitamin and mineral content, and tastes good to boot. Trail mix was designed to be

a lightweight way to carry a high energy food
that would allow distance hikers to carry less
weight and still get the calories they need.
Cheap trail mix is peanuts, raisins and chocolate
chips. I won't knock cheap trail mix as a snack in
your kit. A good, high quality trail mix is a better
idea, but either one will be a good way to keep
your energy up, and since they taste good they'll
help keep your morale up as well. Just watch the
amount of salt in some brands. Or make your
own to be 100% sure what you're getting.

51. Canned fruits and vegetables. Canned foods
    have a very long shelf life. If you already eat
    canned fruits and vegetables, all you need to do
    here is buy a few extra cans when you're at the
    grocery store. You don't even need to buy them
    all at once. A couple of extra cans each trip
    placed into storage instead of the pantry and
    before you know it you'll be stocked up. Once
    you have three to five days' worth of canned
    fruits and vegetables, then the next time you go
    to the store place the freshly bought cans in
    storage, and bring the stored cans to the pantry.
    This will ensure your reserved supply doesn't
    expire. Check your expiration dates often, and
    use foods with the earliest expiration dates first.

52. If you don't generally eat canned fruits and vegetables, consider buying some for just for your preparation supplies. Check the expiration dates before buying, and look for something that will last a year or more. When the cans in your reserve get to be within three to six months of their expiration dates either make an exception and eat the food, or consider donating it to a local food pantry or homeless shelter. Just be sure to do so before it expires.

53. Can your own fruits and vegetables. If you're worried about preservatives, or want to be sure you have organic non-GMO fruits and vegetables in your stock, consider canning your own. I will include some basic home canning tips at the end of this book. If you want to know more than that, you can get a book on canning or even just go online and look up recipes. I highly recommend using only the USDA or other professional food safety guidelines when canning.

54. Canned meats. I know that even the words "canned meat" may make some of you shudder, and others are just fine with it. There are a lot of different canned meats out there these days.

There are canned hams, canned tuna and salmon, canned chicken, the list is pretty long, actually. And it doesn't have to be a traditional "can" either. There are things now like shelf stable foil packs of tuna fish with special recipe seasonings or sauces. Just as with fruits and veggies, if this is a part of your regular shopping list, just buy a few extra next time you go out. If it's not your normal diet, consider buying some just for your preparedness kit. Again, use or donate them before they expire.

55. Canned full meals. Now, I don't think you can buy a canned three course gourmet meal, at least not yet. But canned stews, soups, chili, spaghetti and similar one dish meals are available in a wide variety out there. Even if you have the world's most discerning palate or you are the world's pickiest eater a can of beef stew is going to sound delicious around the forty-eight hour mark. Again, if the only way you will eat these foods is during a survival scenario, donate them to a charity of some sort a few months before they expire. Worst case scenario, you become a slightly better citizen and help someone in your community every few months.

At least if something does happen, you'll be
ready to eat.

56. As with fruits and veggies, you can can your own
meals as well. Soups, stews, chili and even
spaghetti are completely home can-able. Of
course, most charities won't accept home
canned foods, so you will either have to eat it or
discard it after about a year (USDA recommends
keeping home canned foods no more than a
year, grandma on the other hand kept it as long
as the lid didn't pop).

57. Don't forget the baby! If you have a very young
child you will need to stock up on baby food,
formula or cereal as well. Remember though, in
the case of very young children, what they eat
can change very quickly. The transition from
formula to cereal to smooth foods to chunky
foods happens faster than any of these things
expire. Make sure you keep the reserves up to
date with what baby is eating these days. If you
feed your baby homemade baby food, either
prepare and can some food for the baby, or
choose a high quality off the shelf stage
appropriate food to have just in case of
emergencies. Again, if you never need it,

consider yourself lucky and then pass the luck along by donating to the appropriate organizations.

58. Once again, don't forget Fido and Fluffy. Changing your pets' food can often lead to stomach issues. If at all possible, keep extra of the exact food that you normally feed your animals on hand. Just as with your own food, keep an eye on expiration dates, and rotate the stock often.

Hygiene and Other Concerns

One of the things that often gets forgotten in disaster preparations is hygiene and bathroom concerns. We get so used to running water being available on demand that we really aren't ready to live without it. I already mentioned that your safe place should be near a bathroom if at all possible. Now let's talk about what to do if it's not possible to be near a bathroom, or if there is no running water in that bathroom. Let's face it, no one is going to hold it for three days.

The Tips

59. Have plenty of hand sanitizer in your kit. Normally I'm not a fan of hand sanitizer. It is not as effective as plain old soap and hot water, and it only removes germs, not dirt. But when washing your hands properly is not an option, use sanitizer to help give you a fighting chance against bacteria and contamination. Before sanitizing, to remove dirt try using baby wipes (see next).

60. Get a pack or two of baby wipes. If you feel
awkward buying baby wipes, they also sell them
as "bath wipes" or "body wipes" or a few other
names. Whatever you want to call them, buy a
couple packs of waterless wash wipes. After a
day or two without a shower you're really going
to want these. The crotch, armpits and feet are
especially important to keep clean as these areas
stay warm and trap sweat which creates an
environment in which bacteria thrive. This is also
why these areas get to smelling bad before the
rest of our bodies as well. Check these wipes
from time to time when you're checking the rest
of the kit to be sure they haven't dried out.
Along with these have paper towels and facial
tissues on hand as well.

61. Consider a dry shampoo. Don't let the name fool
you, this is effective for the whole body, not just
hair. If you don't want to buy dry shampoo, then
it is easily made at home. It is simply equal parts
cornstarch and baking soda. There are pure
cornstarch baby powders out there now. Read
the label to be sure that's what you're getting.
Or buy a simple box of cornstarch. Mix well with
the baking soda, and ideally store in a shaker
type bottle (like the kind baby powder comes in).

You can add several drops of essential oils as well to smell nicer and feel better about yourself. If you can find cedar oil not only does it smell nice, it repels many types of insects as well. To use it just rub it into your hair down to the scalp, and all over your body, especially the crotch, armpits and feet (as mentioned above). It will absorb sweat and oils, can brush away dirt and will work as a deodorant as well. Check this from time to time to be sure it hasn't clumped up, especially in humid areas. Also, baking soda absorbs odors from the air around it. You should probably replace this after six to twelve months at most. A foot note here, dry shampoo is great for use on your pets between baths as well. I have a Newfoundland dog, and they say not to bathe her in winter, as the oils in her coat keep her waterproof and help with cold resistance (she will literally swim in icy water just for fun). I use dry shampoo on her all winter to keep her from stinking up the house and prevent her hair matting without taking away her natural waterproofing.

62. Make sure you have trash bags. Keep all of your trash, and especially food and bathroom waste in plastic bags, and tie those bags off to prevent

spilling and help trap odors in. Store these bags as far from yourself and your food as possible, and well out of the reach of kids and pets that might play with them. Consider disposable plates, bowls and flatware as well. I know they're wasteful, but doing the dishes without running water is tough.

63. If you know a disaster is coming, fill your bathtub with water. This water is not for drinking, since often bathtubs harbor bacteria (even though you clean it) and trace amounts of cleaning chemicals. Also, once that water has been standing in that tub for a day or two even a tiny amount of bacteria may have grown into a dangerous colony capable of making us sick. No, this water is for the toilet.

64. Keep a two gallon bucket by the toilet somewhere. If you have no running water, you can still flush your toilet by dumping one to two gallons of water into the toilet. Scoop a bucket full of water from the tub, and pour it quickly into the toilet after using it. This should cause the toilet to flush.

65. If you can't get your safe place to be near a bathroom, or if you didn't have enough warning

to fill your bathtub with water, there are other options. These require prior planning and purchasing, but you should consider them seriously for your kit. This is especially true if you have a purpose built shelter (such as a tornado shelter or storm cellar) that doesn't have toilet facilities.

66. Get a camp toilet. The simplest of these is basically a five gallon buck with a toilet seat like lid. Usually they have bags to use to line the bucket with. After use, you tie off the bag and put in a new one. Keep these bags as far from yourself, your food, your pets and your children as you can. Follow the directions on your portable toilet. Or...

67. Improvise a portable toilet by lining a bucket or even an empty toilet with trash bags. After use tie them off tightly and store away from sleeping areas, food, kids and pets.

68. Get a composting toilet. A step up from a bucket and bag toilet, composting toilets are meant to be used dry. Many have a bucket or drawer you can slide out to empty. Again, follow the manufacturer's instructions, and store any waste properly. This can be especially handy in an

unplumbed basement or tornado shelter. Some people are even using them for daily use these days to avoid adding to sewage issues or as part of an off-grid living plan.

69. Whatever method you choose, don't forget the bath tissue. Keep an extra pack in your kit so you don't run out before the stores reopen.

Section 2

Being Prepared at Work or School

So the thought of getting labeled as a prepper or being called paranoid by our coworkers or fellow students isn't particularly a pleasant idea. Besides, every workplace is required to have an emergency plan, right? Well, no they're not. In the US OSHA has a set of regulations that determines whether or not employers must have an action plan, and what that plan must entail. Some require large scale plans, others are smaller scale. Still others, though rare exceptions, aren't required to have a plan at all.

If you are not aware of your company's (or school's) emergency action plan, then either they don't have one, or they have failed at one of the most important steps in an emergency action plan, which is of course, making everyone aware of the emergency action plan. If your company has a safety specialist or safety manager then that is probably the person who knows the plan. Ask them if they have one, and if you can get a copy of it. If they don't have one, maybe you should be looking into why not.

Workplace Preparations

Whether or not your company has a plan already, it's still a good idea to make a plan for yourself. Don't worry, we're not going to make you look crazy. Remember the whole point of this book is to take a common sense approach.

The good news here is that workplace disaster preparation is a much smaller process than home disaster preparation. Most often a workplace emergency is very short lived. Of course, if you work in the medical or emergency response fields this is not true, but then again in those fields disaster response is a big part of the job and plans are generally already in place. Again, if you are not aware of your company's action plan, find out why.

If you are not in the emergency services or healthcare fields, then your best plan of action is really just not to go to work if there is an impending disaster. Of course, sometimes we don't have a choice, and other times we don't have the advanced warning. The most likely disaster to keep us caught at work is a sudden unexpected snowstorm that closes the roads, or a flash flooding situation that blocks your way home. Of course tornadoes, earth quakes, terrorist attacks...these are all possibilities as well, but they are possibilities that are much less likely. This means most often, if we do end up stuck at work, it will probably be for 24 hours or less. As stated previously it usually takes three days to die from dehydration, and three weeks without food. This means in theory we could probably survive at work with almost no preparations at all. But let's not take that chance.

The Tips

70. Know more than one way to and from work. Know several. Know a hundred! Sure you can let your GPS recalculate the route every time you pass by another closed off road. But you could save time by already knowing your alternate routes. If your area has marked snow emergency or detour routes, know them and which of them pass close to both work and home. These are usually the last routes to close and the first to reopen.

71. Remember those medications mentioned back in Tip 12? Make sure to have a few days' supply with you at work or school. Or anytime you are anywhere, really. Whether you carry them with

you, or keep some in your locker or desk, just so long as you have them. And make sure you don't let them expire.

72. If you are allowed to do so, and have a place to store it, the best thing to do is bring a backpack to work with everything you need for a day or two of preparations. The backpacks with a hydration bladder would be a great choice as they are designed to carry water already. Just remember to keep the bladder and straw clean in accordance with the manufacturer's instructions and change the water (if you're not drinking it) daily.

73. Know how much water the backpack holds. It is likely that it will not hold a full gallon. Throwing a few bottles of water into the backpack will help bring you up to the one gallon target. The simple truth is, so long as you can store it or carry it, you can never have too much water.

74. Put some food in your backpack. The same shelf stable foods we talked about for the home can go in your backpack. You're probably already bringing a lunch every day. Adding just a few cans or foil packs of food will give you plenty to hold out for a day or two. Meal replacement

bars are another option. Just note the calories on them. Some are designed for dieting, and therefore have very few calories. These aren't the ones you're going to want in a survival situation. You want high calorie foods here. High calorie foods will give you the energy you need in a smaller package. They may leave you feeling hungry, but the total calories will keep you going.

75. Pack an extra coat. A hat and gloves aren't a bad idea either, especially if it's winter time. If the power goes out in your building, it may get pretty cold. Consider packing a survival blanket as well. A Mylar survival blanket folds up to about the size of a deck of playing cards and yet can keep you so warm that occasionally people have gotten burned by them. This is rare, but if you feel hot, uncover for a bit to be safe.

76. Pack a flashlight. Check the batteries often.

77. If you're not allowed to bring a backpack then hopefully you have someplace to store stuff at work. A desk drawer or a locker can become your workplace disaster preparedness storage. A lunch box or bag can double up as your kit as

well. If all else fails, stick water bottles and protein bars in your coat pockets.

78. Store water at work. Even if your job site already has water for you in the form of water coolers or free bottled water, it never hurts to have your own water supply. You shouldn't need more than a gallon at most, and even if you have less you're not likely to feel the effects of severe dehydration in just a day. If you have a desk or a locker, you can easily store a few water bottles and just keep them on hand. If the company provides free bottled water you can even just grab a bottle every day or so and put it aside for emergency use (unless this is expressly forbidden for some reason).

79. Just as mentioned for the backpack, storing some food in your desk or locker is a great idea. This does add one extra concern, though. Be sure to check your wrappers or packaging frequently for any signs that bugs or rodents have gotten at your food. Many workplaces are home to all sorts of critters who would love to snack on your snacks.

80. Have a copy of your emergency phone numbers at work. Be sure to add any daycare, babysitters

or school numbers you may need. Label these numbers clearly as to who is who in case something should happen and someone else besides you needs to make any of those calls.

81. Make sure anyone who might need to get a hold of you in an emergency has numbers at your work besides your cell phone. More and more companies are telling people to leave cell phones in their lockers or in their cars. Your spouse, your child's school, your parents...these people need to know another way to get a hold of you if there should happen to be an emergency of some sort.

82. If you own your own business, and don't work from home you will have to decide how prepared you need to be at work. Do you work when there's bad weather? Even snowstorms or flood warnings in the forecast? If so, and if possible, stockpile your work following the tips I gave for at home. Do you stay home when you expect the weather to get ugly? If you do, then pack a bag as I suggested for work just on the off chance a surprise disaster catches you off guard. Do you have employees...?

83. If you run your own business and you have employees then you should have a disaster readiness plan in place. OSHA has specific guidelines for Emergency Action Plans (EAPs). Make sure you're in compliance, and consider going above and beyond the minimum requirements. A quick online search will find you safety experts and consultants in your area if you need help. If you have just a few employees then you could get a case of MREs or camping meals and a couple cases of water to keep on the site just in case something happens. If you have dozens or hundreds of staff members, you will need to plan bigger. It's the only ethical thing to do.

Section 3

In the Car

So, being trapped in your car isn't something many people think about these days. We tend to take for granted that with cell phones and GPS systems we'll always be able to figure out where we are, and to call someone for help. With roadside service or roadside assistance plans being offered by everyone from triple A and your car dealer to insurance plans and even some jobs it can seem like we're never more than a phone call from being rescued.

Except of course when we have no reception for our phones. Or when the roads have been closed by a state of emergency. Or when the tow truck gets stuck in the snow as well. Or the roadside service provider informs you there are literally ten people ahead of you, and it's going to be 12 to 24 hours before they can get to you...

In January of 2016 winter storm Jonas slammed the Eastern US. Over a hundred motorists were stuck in cars on I-75 in Kentucky for almost 24 hours, and hundreds more were trapped on the Pennsylvania Turnpike for nearly 30 hours. The National Guard brought them food and water, and in some cases put gas in the cars so that the motorists could keep them running for heat. But what if the National Guard hadn't been activated? What if they couldn't get to the stuck cars? What if you weren't in that pile up, but rather off on some side road where nobody knew you were there?

The Tips

84. Before we even get into the kit, let's start with the vehicle itself. Inspect your vehicle regularly. Check for damage, unusual tire wear, broken exhaust pipes and other hazards. Make sure the vehicle is road worthy at all times. If you're not good with cars, have a mechanic do it for you. Often if you ask to have this done with another service such as an oil change or a brake job there will be little to no additional charge. Don't trust that your once a year state inspection (if you have one) is enough. Check it out at the start of every season as a bare minimum. A well maintained vehicle is less likely to break down, and slightly less likely to slide of the road as well.

85. Learn (or re-learn, or remember) safe and defensive driving techniques. Look for classes in your area that will teach you or refresh your memory on driving safely or in bad weather. Taking these classes may even get you a break on your auto insurance. Check with your insurer to see. Avoiding a pile up altogether or maintaining control in a skid could be the difference between needing rescued and simply needing to change your shorts.

86. Always keep your fuel tank full. There are many reasons to never let your fuel gauge get below half. It helps prevent any water or dirt in the bottom of the tank from getting sucked up into the motor. It reduces the amount of fuel evaporation in the tank, which prevents fumes escaping to the atmosphere. This saves money and the environment (a little, but it adds up). It prevents condensation inside the empty tank, since there's no room for water vapor to get in. It helps prevent the fuel tank from rusting as well. It prevents you from being late to work when you don't have to gas up in the morning when you already got a late start. For our purposes though, it ensures that if you get stuck

and have to wait before you can move again, you will have fuel to run the vehicle for heat.

87. A kit for your car is going to have to be flexible. It will need to change as the seasons change, and will need to grow or shrink with the number of passengers and the length of the trip planned. Or, you could just build the maximum kit you might need for a full load of passengers in any possible conditions and leave it in the car if you have the space. That would be my recommendation, but it may not always be practical for everyone. If that is the case for you, be prepared to adjust your kit often.

88. Another option is a "modular" kit. In a modular kit, each passenger would have their own kit, generally in the form of a bag or backpack that contains their parts of the kit. This would be independent of the actual vehicle kit, and contain food, water, weather appropriate clothes, blanket(s) and a flashlight for each person. Mylar emergency blankets or even Mylar emergency sleeping bags are a good choice here. They fold up to about the size of a deck of cards, and yet they can keep you incredibly warm. The vehicle kit would contain everything that the

individuals don't carry for themselves. You may notice that the individual kit is essentially the same pack you should already be carrying to work or school, so I won't spend more time on it.

89. Remember Tips 12 and 71? I don't mean to get repetitive, but this is a big deal. Always have extras of any medications that you may need along with you when you are traveling. Even if the trip is supposed to be short. Remember Gilligan and the gang? That was supposed to be a three hour tour, folks.

90. Have a shovel, an axe or hatchet, and some kind of traction material (the last is more for winter) in the car. Jumper cables, a tow rope and a come-along (ratchetting hand winch) can be very useful as well. And know how to use them. Know how to work the come-along, know how to dig a hole and know how to chop wood. These skills can be useful when you get stuck. And know where on your car it is safe to tie onto. Here's a hint, it is not the plastic bumper cover.

91. Get a fire extinguisher for your vehicle. Just like in tip 11, make it a dry chemical ABC type extinguisher, and again, know how to use it. If you do have a fire in the vehicle, don't get back

in! Fires can smolder undetected and then flare back up, and the toxic smoke can fill the cabin and linger long after you put the fire out.

92. Know how to get your vehicle unstuck. Sometimes your best option may actually be to figure out how to get yourself unstuck. There are three basic scenarios where your car could end up stuck. The first is snow and ice. You slide from the main roadway and get stuck, either in deep snow or on slick ice, and the vehicle simply will not move. The second is mud or water. Mud or water washes over the roadway (or you are out in the woods four wheeling) and you get stuck in deep mud, or swamp your motor with water. The third is the soft shoulder. You pull off the side of the road to wait out the storm, or use the bathroom. Suddenly you realize that the car is sinking in the soft dirt around you. In normal circumstances, this is when you call for a tow. During a disaster, you may need to be able to get yourself out. Have the equipment in the vehicle to deal with common hazards.

93. As a footnote, never, ever drive into unfamiliar waters or even familiar waters during unfamiliar conditions. You may ford a stream in the woods

every time you go out there, but if the water looks unusual, or the weather is bad, stay away. You may know that the water is usually only an inch or two deep when it washes over a familiar road known for flooding during even small rains, but looks can be deceiving. Muddy waters may hide deep holes, or the roadway beneath may have even been washed away. Even if the water is no deeper than usual, if it is moving faster than normal, everything can change. It takes surprising little water to move a vehicle if the circumstances are right. You could be washed away before you even realize what's happening.

94. Is it winter? A shovel and some traction material will get you out of most snow and ice conditions. Kitty litter is a surprisingly affordable and effective traction material. Dig out any snow that is between your tires and the direction you are attempting to travel. Spread a layer of kitty litter on the ice in front of the tires, including packing some in against the tires where they meet the ground. Oddly, shoving newspapers under the tires is often very effective as well. Either way, be sure to remove any deep snow from between the car and where you want to go first, and don't mash the gas. Let the car idle in

drive or reverse, and simply lift your foot off of the brake. If you have to give it gas, do so smoothly and slowly.

95. Stuck in the mud? Again, dig out as much as you can of the material around the tires down to the bottom of the rubber. Trying to go forward, dig in from of the tires. Trying to reverse? Dig behind. Use your axe or hatchet to chop up some braches and shove them under the tire for traction. If there's large gravel nearby, trying shoveling that in under the tires as well. And again, idle in gear, don't mash the gas.

96. In both of the above scenarios if the methods listed fail, you may be able to winch yourself out. If you have a winch on your vehicle, hopefully you already know how to use it. If you don't have a winch, a hand powered one (usually called a come-along) could be an option. In both of these cases, you need to know ahead of time how to use it. Take the time to learn before you have to do it in bad conditions. Also, especially with the hand winch, you are probably going to end up wet, dirty and cold by the time you are done. You're going to have to crawl on the ground in that mud, water or snow to attach it

to the vehicle frame. The bumper or body panels simply won't do. Evaluate your situation carefully, and be sure that you can get out this way before attempting it, or you're likely to just make your situation worse. Being cold, wet, muddy and still stuck is not going to improve things at all.

97. Have food and water in the car. Enough for two or three days per person, at least. Everyone can carry these themselves if you're using the modular kit plan. Even then, having some extra in the vehicle wouldn't hurt. This is the one time I will recommend shelf stable meals such as military MREs or packaged hunter's meals as an option. I personally still prefer standard canned and boxed foods, but the MREs have their place. Outdoor stores, camping stores, hunting supply stores, and a surprising number of gun shops carry these. They are much more convenient for storing in the vehicle, and for moving back and forth. While they are not meant to be frozen, they do tolerate freezing better than cans or jars do, and they generally have a flameless heater packed in the kit with them. If you choose this option, be sure to follow the directions carefully on the heaters, and don't use them in an

airtight, or nearly airtight space (like inside of your car). And again, NOT freeze dried meals. These require way too much of your water, and as mentioned before, you need the water way more than you need the food. If you park in a climate controlled garage overnight, everything can be left in the car. Otherwise, it is highly recommended that you take everything inside whenever possible if the car is going to sit in below freezing temps for an extended period of time.

98. Flashlights for everybody! Seriously, I know I'm getting repetitive here, but everyone gets a flashlight. One in each person's modular bag. Two or three in the car kit. Another in the glove box. Flashlights can be used to see where you're going. They can be used as a distress beacon to flag down other vehicles. They can be used to warn traffic of your presence so you don't get run over in the dark. The light reassures adults and children alike when you're sitting in a dark vehicle. They are too easy and too affordable to justify not having one.

99. Don't count on the vehicle to keep you warm. If you were in an accident, the vehicle may not

run. Even if it does run, you should try to run it as little as possible. You may need the fuel to get yourself out when the conditions change. Also, make sure there is nothing blocking your exhaust. Get out and dig any snow, mud or debris away from your exhaust pipes. Any blockage at all could cause carbon monoxide to back up into the vehicle's cabin area, and since you can't see, smell or taste it, you would never know anything was wrong until it was too late.

100.   If you do run the vehicle, keep at least one window open a little bit while it is running to allow any exhaust gasses to escape. Don't sleep with the vehicle running (make sure at least one person is awake), and I know it sounds crazy (especially if you're in the cold) but open a door or a window all the way for at least one minute every hour or two. This will allow the air in the vehicle to exchange with outside air, ensuring the oxygen isn't getting used up, and again, allowing any exhaust gasses to escape completely, being replaced with fresh air.

101.   Have emergency blankets in the car. Again, even if everyone has their own blankets, having extra in the car is a good idea. If you're packing

the vehicle kit and not using the modular plan, pack extra blankets. If you're stranded for any length of time, you may not be able to run the vehicle even if there is no damage. Hanging blankets over the windows and as much of the interior as possible will keep it considerably warmer in the vehicle.

102.   Have a glass punch in the car. Breaking the window of a car is actually surprisingly difficult. Modern cars have crumple zones designed to absorb the impact of a collision. Frequently these result in the front and/or back of the car being pushed towards the center. This can sometimes jam the doors. You could also be pushed against, or slide into a bank, berm, wall, etc. that stops you from opening your doors. If your power has failed, and you can't get the windows down and the doors won't open, breaking a window may be your only option. The small point of a glass punch focuses the force of a blow in a tiny area, and makes it much easier to break the window. I won't suggest practicing this one, as replacing windows is expensive. I will say this; make sure everyone in the vehicle faces away from the window to be broken. Closing your eyes and covering up with a

blanket or coat is a good idea as well. Then simply slam the point of the punch into the center of the glass.

103.   Have a strap cutter (seat belt cutter) in the car as well. A strap cutter has a groove to catch the belt, and the blade is tucked back out of the way to protect your hands. If you are in a situation where you can't get at the buckle of your seatbelt (or someone else's seatbelt) and must get out of the car quickly, this could make all the difference. I have an EMS folding knife in my car. I keep it in the center console so it's always handy. The maker of the knife designed it so there is a groove cut in the handle. When the blade is closed, this groove makes it into a strap cutter. There is also a glass breaker punch on the end of the handle. Of course, again, check your laws and know the rules where you are traveling. Here in Pennsylvania the law says a knife is a tool. It's legal to have it on me or in the car. In many states, blade length determines if it's a tool or a weapon, and in some states it's just outright illegal to carry a knife at all. If you live in one of those states, I'd suggest moving. Or buy a dedicated strap cutter, whichever works for you.

Be warned: A good kit will contain everything you need to survive a few days trapped in your car, as well as everything you might need to help you "self-recover" the vehicle, that is, to get your own vehicle unstuck from snow, mud or a soft shoulder of the road without outside assistance. This means things like shovels, axes, knives and ropes. Preppers, survivalists and those who are ready for anything tend to call this kit an "EDC", or Every Day Carry. Some law enforcement agencies however may look at this kit and see a crime kit instead. After all, ropes, knives, shovels, axes and blankets may be what you need to survive, but that same list could be used by a serial killer to capture, contain and dispose of their victims. Placing a copy of this book or the FEMA preparedness guide in the bag might help, but the life of a law enforcement officer can sometimes make people cynical. It's not their fault; the side of people they see leads some of them to always assume the worst.

Another word of caution: As with everything, know the laws where you are and where you're going. As always, I will point out that many people make a gun a part of their kit. This is entirely a question of personal choice. Just be sure to know if it is legal to transport a gun in your car where you live, where you're going, and everywhere in between. And for crying out loud, if you haven't already, please, please take a gun safety course. Even if you don't own a gun, it will never hurt to know how to handle one safely. Also, check if it's legal to have an axe, machete, knife, etc. in your car or on your person. I don't know of anywhere that these items are illegal to transport in your vehicle, but I haven't study every state, county, city, etc. when it comes to the law. Plus, new things are outlawed almost daily it seems. Know whether or not you're even allowed to self-recover your vehicle in your area. There are places where it is required that you notify police of any accident or incident that results in a vehicle becoming stuck.

Bonus Section – Canning and Food Storage Tips

So I promised you some tips and tricks for canning food at home. That's what this section is for. I won't really go into recipes too much, since the range of things that can be canned is incredibly diverse. I'm also not going to go in depth into the canning process, either. It varies from recipe to recipe anyway. No, this is just going to be a brief overview of canning and food storage in general.

Many people these days are worried about what is in their food, and with good reason. Chemical preservatives, artificial flavors, artificial sweeteners and genetically modified foods are all we seem to hear about these days. Our grandparents and great grandparents never used monosodium glutamate or triphosphorous-dioxide when the canned their food, and they kept it in the cellar for the whole year, sometimes longer. Why do we need all of this now? Well, we don't. A little while back consumers decided that they wanted foods that looked or tasted fresher, they wanted sponge cakes that don't go stale, or pickles that stay bright and vivid green. And through the wonders of chemistry, they got it. No one cared or checked if those chemicals might kill us in the long run. If you didn't die as soon as you ate it, it was deemed safe.

Soon the old ways of making it from scratch or preserving it yourself fell to the wayside in favor of fast, easy and affordable. And since no one was staying home anymore, who had time to pick fresh fruits, clean all those veggies, and slave over a hot stove to put it all up for the winter? No one, that's who, so we all started living on processed, chemically preserved garbage. And if you're ok with that, well then good for you. I'm not giving up my bacon wrapped deep fried Oreo stuffed Twinkies any time soon either.

But I don't eat them every day. And I have been known to bake my own cakes, cure my own bacon and fry my own Oreos from time to time. I also make my own pickles, jams, jelly, stews and soups, spice rubs, tomato sauces, etc., etc... And people often ask me where I find the time. I usually answer that by asking them who got kicked off of that reality show last night? When they answer, I tell them, see, I didn't watch it. That one hour of TV for you was half a dozen jars of pickles for me. If I worked for an hour at my job, I wouldn't make enough money to buy 6 big jars of good pickles. But for about an hour's worth of work and five or six dollars' worth of ingredients I have six big jars of delicious, chemical free pickles. A trip to the farmers' market and a weekend in the kitchen fills my pantry with jelly, applesauce, jam, and canned fruit for what averages out to about a third of the store price, and I know, heck I handpicked, every ingredient used. Both literally and figuratively.

Now, the initial cost to get started canning can be a little high. If you want to be able to can everything you could imagine, you're going to need a pressure cooker with a gauge, jar racks, lids, jar tongs, jar funnels, ladles, and whatever else I am forgetting in order to get started. But if you can regularly all of that will pay for itself in a very short time. Plus, you will have better food. Now, there is some debate about nutrition loss during canning versus flash freezing, however the USDA claims that fruits and vegetables canned within 12 hours of picking are actually healthier than the fresh produce in the grocery store. This is due to the fact that vitamin content and quality of produce begins to drop as soon as it is picked, and the stuff listed as "fresh" at the supermarket has been picked days, or sometimes weeks before you buy it. Canning quickly after picking preserves almost all of the nutritional content. Yes, the high temps involved can remove some vitamins, most notably A, D and Thiamine. But preserving everything else makes the heat damage a minimal cost in my opinion.

So, what exactly is canning? Well canning is the process of sealing foods against oxygen and contaminants. This stops the ripening and rotting processes, prevents spoilage from yeast, mold and other microorganisms, and preserves the nutritional content of the food. It does not, however protect the food from many anaerobic bacteria, such as our old friend botulism. For that we need another way of protecting the food. This is done through one of two methods during the canning process.

The first method is making the food (or choosing food that already is) acidic. A pH level of 4.6 or lower means the food is acidic enough to prevent botulism from growing. This is done by using acidic foods, or by adding acid, usually in the form of lemon juice, citric acid or vinegar. The other method is by superheating the food to make it sterile. Superheating means bringing the food to a temperature of about 250° F (about 121°C) for a specific amount of time (check the recipes for specific food's recommended time). To achieve this temperature without burning the food, we put the food into a sealed jar and then submerge it in boiling water.

The problem with this process is that water boils at 212°F (100°C), and simply cannot be heated past the boiling point at normal atmospheric pressure. An interesting fact of physics is that under normal earth conditions water can never be hotter than boiling or colder than freezing without outside influences of pressure or chemical contamination with things like salt or alcohol (antifreeze). Higher atmospheric pressure raises the temperature at which water boils, and lower pressure lowers the boiling point. In the vacuum of space water will actually boil into a vapor, and then the vapor will freeze into a sort of snow. But I digress... Raising the pressure by putting the water and the jars of food into a pressure cooker allows us to achieve the desired temperature for sterilizing the food in the jars.

By using either method, you create a sterilized, safe, shelf stable food product that will last for a year or more (the USDA recommends no more than one year) without chemical preservatives or ingredients created in some lab somewhere. And that means it creates healthy food we can store on a shelf for our emergency plan. Food we chose ourselves, with ingredients we picked and recipes we know we like, and that doesn't require any refrigeration. What's more, in most cases it's actually perfectly safe to eat right out of the jar with no additional cooking (check your canning recipes and label your food accordingly to be safe). You could even put it all in single serving pint or half pint jars so that everyone could choose their own meals, and when it's time to use it up before it expires, you could take it to work or school as your lunch.

So exactly what can you can? Almost anything, really. If you can't find a recipe for canning something, look for something similar and use that recipe. Can't find a recipe for canning chili? Try the recipe for meat sauce. As long as you can get the food packed in a way that leaves no air (hence the use of liquids to can fruits and veggies), and then process it correctly, it will be safe to can.

This is also a great way to save money as well. Is there a big sale of stew meat? Buy a few pounds, make a huge pot of stew and can it for later. Does the farmers' market have a huge basket of carrots for just a few dollars due to a bumper crop? Take them home, clean them up, put them in a jar with boiling water and seal them up. You'll have carrots available all winter without paying the higher prices once the cold weather hits. Do the kids like their pb&j sandwiches? Fresh fruit, a pack or two of low sugar pectin, an hour's work and you've got a year's supply of low sugar, no high fructose corn syrup jelly. Do you like applesauce? Do you avoid it because there are so many chemicals or so much added sugar, and the "healthy" brands are so expensive? If you know how to make mashed potatoes, you already know how to make applesauce. Pro tip, I add a pinch of ginger and a pinch of ground clove. Everyone loves it so much that's it's hardly worth canning. They eat it before it has a chance to spoil no matter how much I make.

Hunters, instead of freezing your harvest, cook it up and then can it. Venison or rabbit stew ready to go at a moment's notice until next season. It'll last longer, there'll be no freezer burn, and it doesn't take up as much space in the deep freezer.

Afterword

I sincerely hope you are one of the lucky ones who never have to face a disaster. If you do ever have to face one, I hope that this book and the steps included in it will help you downgrade that disaster to a mere inconvenience. At the very least, I hope this will help prevent it from becoming a full on tragedy somehow.

Please go online and download FEMA's preparedness guide and study it as well. I don't think you will find anything in this book that directly conflicts with that guide, and the simple truth is that you can never have too much information when it comes to being prepared. Look for the FEMA courses online as well, and consider taking the certification tests they offer. Make sure to include everyone around you in your planning, as well as in your plans.

Again, remember that this book is solely my own opinion, and that it is intended as a starting point for you. It is by no means the be-all and end-all of being prepared, but I do believe that it is a good start. It's up to you to take responsibility for your own safety and preparedness, and even if you ignore everything else that I have said, I hope that at least I have inspired you to do that much.